INTERACTIVE **WORKBOOK**

TOUGH TALK TO TENDER HEARTS™

*How to Talk to Children about Sex
and the Risk of Sexual Abuse*

BOOKLOGIX
Alpharetta, GA

The resources contained within this book are provided for informational purposes only and should not be used to replace the specialized training and professional judgment of a healthcare or mental healthcare professional. Angela's Voice and the publisher of this work cannot be held responsible for the use of the information provided. Always consult a licensed mental health professional before making any decision regarding treatment of yourself or others.

Copyright © 2011, 2016, 2023 by Angela's Voice

3rd Edition

All rights reserved. No part of this book may be reproduced or transmitted in any form or by any means, electronic or mechanical, including photocopying, recording, or any information storage and retrieval system, without permission in writing from the author.

ISBN: 978-1-61005-627-4

This ISBN is the property of BookLogix for the express purpose of sales and distribution of this title. The content of this book is the property of the copyright holder only. BookLogix does not hold any ownership of the content of this book and is not liable in any way for the materials contained within. The views and opinions expressed in this book are the property of the Author/Copyright holder, and do not necessarily reflect those of BookLogix.

∞ This paper meets the requirements of ANSI/NISO Z39.48-1992 (Permanence of Paper)

Author, Angela Williams, MFP
Evaluation by Emory Rollins School of Public Health
Design and Illustration by Mark Sandlin
Design production by Felicia Kahn

041923

CONTENTS

Before You Begin _____ 1

Introduction: Why Are Child Sexual Abuse Prevention and Support Important? _____ 2

"The Talk" _____ 5

Empowering Your Children to Establish Their Boundaries _____ 9

Anatomy 101 _____ 13

Potential Signs of Child Sexual Abuse _____ 23

Disclosure _____ 25

References _____ 28

Angela's Voice _____ 30

Join the Angela's Voice Movement _____ 32

Facilitation Guide _____ 33

BEFORE YOU BEGIN

Angela's Voice is always trying to improve our programming, and we need your help! In order to best evaluate the effectiveness of our programs, we ask that you take a survey both before and after going through the curriculum. You can find both tests in the Facilitation Guide as well as online. So before you start reading, go ahead and take the Pretest Evaluation right now!

YOUR OPTIONS FOR EVALUATIONS:

In order to get the evaluations back to us, you can do one of the following:

- **Scan them!** Fill out the evaluations by hand and scan and email them to angela@angelakwilliams.com.
- **Fill them out online!** You can find the evaluations online at:
    — Pretest: https://goo.gl/4tBTMT
    — Post-Test: https://goo.gl/Rj2JWU

INTRODUCTION: WHY ARE CHILD SEXUAL ABUSE PREVENTION AND SUPPORT IMPORTANT?

Tough Talk To Tender Hearts is a workbook that guides adults through the process of talking to children about sexual abuse and its associated risks. Through this book, adults will learn skills that will help them become more confident about their ability to have this often challenging conversation with children at different developmental stages.

WHY A WORKSHOP ON TEACHING CHILDREN ABOUT SEX?

1. Children need clinical information on the biological process and physiological changes to the body.
2. Children need information about sex at an early age as a tool against abuse.
3. Children need information about sex in the context of relationships to introduce the concept of boundaries (1) against abuse and (2) in support of healthy relationships.
4. We live in an overly sexualized society.

THEMES OF TOUGH TALK

Teachable Moments
What are they?
When do they occur?

Responsibilities
Sexual education for your children is your duty.

Normal Development
Children should experience a natural development and timely understanding of sex.

KNOW THIS:
Abuse happens in your neighborhoods.
If you believe your children are not at risk, you may not pay close enough attention, and they may pay a high price.

STATISTICS

Almost anyplace you go, you will find someone who has been sexually abused in his or her lifetime. The numbers are staggering. For the purposes of this workbook, we will focus on childhood sexual abuse.

> - 44% of sexual assault and rape victims are under the age of 18.[2]
> - 7% of girls in grades 5–8 and 12% of girls in grades 9–12 said they had been sexually abused.[3]
> - 3% of boys grades 5–8 and 5% of boys in grades 9–12 said they had been sexually abused.[2]
> - 93% of juvenile sexual assault victims know their attacker.[4]
>   - 34.2% of attackers were family members.
>   - 58.7% were acquaintances.

CONSEQUENCES TO VICTIMS AND SOCIETY

In most cases, children do not understand why sexual advances are wrong; they only know that it doesn't "feel" right. They are not equipped to verbalize to an abuser to stop the action. They must be taught. And if they are not taught, they become easy targets for manipulation.

Children naturally respond to people who give them attention. They don't question the actions because they are naturally trusting of those whom they know. Often, they even trust strangers if the attention feels good. Generally, children want to please adults, so they are obedient, even in the face of confusion and impending fear.

When abuse occurs, a child is left feeling confused and scared about what happened, causing—in most cases—the child to go silent. Perhaps the perpetrator made threats (often against people the child loves) to the child if he or she "told." The ensuing consequences cover a wide range of negative and destructive behaviors and emotions that overlap into the effects on loved ones—and society in general. In many cases, a victim experiences more than one consequence as a child and into adulthood.

---

[2] U.S. Bureau of Justice Statistics, Sex Offenses and Offenders. 1997.
[3] 1998 Commonwealth Fund Survey of the Health of Adolescent Girls. 1998.
[4] U.S. Bureau of Justice Statistics. 2000 Sexual Assault of Young Children as Reported to Law Enforcement. 2000.

Compared to people who have not experienced sexual violence, victims of sexual assault are[5]:

- 3 times more likely to suffer from depression.
- 6 times more likely to suffer from post-traumatic stress disorder.
- 13 times more likely to abuse alcohol.
- 26 times more likely to abuse drugs.
- 4 times more likely to contemplate suicide.

The National Sexual Violence Resource Centers analyzed several studies conducted between 2000 and 2011 concerning the re-victimization of people who have experienced childhood sexual abuse. One article that looked at 128 international scholarly articles found that sexual victimization in childhood increases the likelihood of sexual victimization in adulthood between 2 and 13.7 times.[6] Another found that among female respondents who had reported experiencing a completed rape before the age of eighteen, 35.2% also experienced a completed rape as an adult, compared to 14.2% of women who did not experience rape before age eighteen.[7]

ADVERSE CHILDHOOD EXPERIENCES (ACE) STUDY

The Center for Disease Control and Prevention performed a study on adults to examine the short- and long-term outcomes of childhood abuse, neglect, and other traumatic stressors—adverse childhood experiences (ACE). As the number of ACEs increased, the risk of the following behaviors and "health problems increase[d] in a strong and graded fashion":

- Alcoholism and alcohol abuse
- Chronic Obstructive Pulmonary Disease (COPD)
- Depression
- Fetal Death
- Sexually Transmitted Diseases
- Illicit drug use and smoking
- Liver disease
- Risk for intimate partner violence
- Suicide attempts
- Multiple sex partners
- Ischemic heart disease (IHD)
- Unintended pregnancies

---

[5] World Health Organization. 2002.

[6] U.S. Bureau of Justice Statistics, Sex Offenses and Offenders. 1997.

[7] 1998 Commonwealth Fund Survey of the Health of Adolescent Girls. 1998.

"THE TALK"

WHY TEACH ABOUT SEX?

- Because...We need to provide children with a tool—knowledge—for protection.
- Because...Our children are bombarded with sexual content frequently and prematurely, and we live in an overly sexualized society.
- Because...Curiosity about sex naturally occurs.
- Because...Sex is rarely presented by the world in the context of family values.
- Because...Sex is everywhere. Our responsibility is to be their source of scientifically sound knowledge.
- Because...It is our responsibility, as adults, to keep them safe.

QUESTIONS & REFLECTIONS

- As a child, who did you go to when you had questions about sex?
- Did you get accurate answers?
- If not, how would you have changed your experience?
- From whom should your children get answers about sex?
- Now, based on your reflections, think about your children and how they may be thinking about sex. What are their needs?

TEACHABLE MOMENTS AND THE "TALK"

What is "the talk?" The talk involves layers of conversations about sex, starting from a young age for as long as your child needs to talk. Note the plural! Most parents believe that waiting until puberty is the time for the whole story about sex, but children are not ready (or capable) of grappling with everything about sex all at one time. Nor are they interested in getting the talk in one sitting. When your children ask questions, focus on the question at hand without elaboration. Take note that your cues may shift based on the questions your children ask. Below are some helpful tips to consider before having "the talk."

- **Lay a strong and stable foundation.** Pacing the talks in tandem with your children's natural curiosity establishes a foundation of trust and open lines of communication. As more complex issues arise, you will continue to build on the groundwork, trust, and relationship that have developed over time.

- **Take advantage of teachable moments.** What are teachable moments? They are times when you can discuss sex in a non-threatening and natural way, so that when children have questions, they will come to you. Be alert for opportunities. Everyday activities are the easiest and most logical times during which sex discussions can occur. Activities that offer good opportunities for sex conversations include doctor visits, outings, and stories in the news. Talking frequently creates a relaxed and normal avenue for a healthy conversation about a difficult subject.

> Equipped with a healthy understanding of sex, children will also sense the warning signs when they are threatened with abuse.

How can we take natural, ordinary scenarios and turn them into teachable moments? Keep in mind that children parrot not only our words, but our actions as well. If you begin appropriate and honest discussions around sex early in your child's development, your child will grow up with a healthy understanding about what sex is and how it is designed for pleasure and procreation in an adult relationship.

Sex is everywhere! All one has to do is turn on the TV, watch a movie, surf the Internet, or open a magazine, and sexual content, in one form or another, is right in front of our eyes—and our children's eyes. They are exposed to much more than is healthy for them and more than they can process. Sex in the media is not presented in ways that follow the normal and natural development of sexual discovery in children—too much too soon is overwhelming. If they don't ask questions at those moments, the questions surely will come when you least expect them. And children will persist in asking if they don't receive honest answers.

Teachable moments are valuable times to build trust and to educate your child. Watch for clues to initiate conversations that may come from experiences, circumstances, or your child. As your child matures, you will be able to gradually increase the scope and depth of the topic. When you become sensitive to the moments when sex talks are appropriate and warranted, you must take hold of those opportunities, stop what you are doing, and engage with your child on this important topic over the period of your child's development.

FAMILY VALUES AND YOUR STORY

Encourage your family values during sex talks. The most obvious and meaningful way to do this is to tell the story of how you (the parents) met, dated, fell in love, decided to marry, and then started your family. In other family scenarios, like a single parent family or adoption, explain how much they were wanted and the excitement of their arrival. Adapt this according to your story and their developmental stages. By telling the story that is personal to them, you instill:

1. **Implicit boundaries**
2. **Their sense of belonging, value, and worth**
3. **A sense of their place in the world**

BRAINSTORM

Think of some natural experiences where the subject of sex might arise. What might your responses be when:

- You walk in on your child playing doctor with another child?
- Your child walks into your bedroom unexpectedly while you are being intimate with your partner?

Think of other such normal and casual experiences where sex talks can occur and share your ideas with others.

REVIEW: TEACHABLE MOMENTS OCCUR...

Over years, increasing the scope and depth of topics as the child grows.

- During non-threatening moments making talks easier during difficult times.
- During everyday activities that present discussion topics.
- In relaxed and casual conversations.
- To reinforce family values and build trust.

DUTIES AND RESPONSIBILITIES

All parents and legal guardians have the duty to teach their children about relationships and sex. Many, though, don't realize that sex education is a multi-pronged process; it isn't just about the clinical description of intercourse.

Sex education involves discussions about physical and emotional boundaries, healthy relationships, modesty, respect, love, and compassion. While modeling these behaviors speaks volumes to our children, conversations about the myriad of issues surrounding them are, nevertheless, vital. Children need to be able to ask their questions and get honest answers without fear of reprisal or embarrassment. Consider the following points prior to beginning these discussions.

- Be the primary source of your child's sex education at an early age.
- Answer questions when they are asked, not when it is more convenient for you.
- Understand and instill appropriate boundaries.
- Support your child's feeling of empowerment by modeling your boundaries.
- Allow them the right to refuse affection, a kiss, or a hug.
- Allow them the freedom to ask questions.
- Always believe your child.

EMPOWERING YOUR CHILDREN TO ESTABLISH THEIR BOUNDARIES

REJECTION OR EMPOWERMENT?

Boundaries are the emotional and physical space that we place between ourselves and others.

Remember those unwelcomed hugs, wet smooches, and pinches on the cheeks? If your child backs away, that's okay. Support your child! Don't make excuses to Aunt Bertha for your child's reaction or decision. Let Aunt Bertha know that your child is learning about personal boundaries, personal power, and their right to say "no" to unwanted touch.

Ask yourself:

- Are you concerned about rejecting or offending the adult? Or...
- Are you protecting, supporting, and empowering your child?

THE "NO!" VOICE

Many of us grew up being told to listen to adults or people in authority and to obey them. We were taught not to argue for fear of being punished. The last thing on earth we wanted to do was get in trouble for bad behavior because we talked back or refused to do what we were told. Let us rethink this old-fashioned technique of parenting. Within reason, teach your child about their "NO!" voice. It is strong, loud, definite, and it has the power to fend off a potential attacker, particularly one whom the child knows.

- Teach them: "Honey, it's okay for you to say loudly, 'No! Stop that!'"
- Tell them: "You have my permission to shout 'No! Stop that!' if someone is trying to touch you in a way that is not okay with you." A child's "NO!" voice has the power to stop abuse and create a sense of empowerment within the child.

MORE RESPONSIBILITY

Demonstrate boundaries and intervene quickly when you see or hear anything inappropriate. Maintain a home environment that respects privacy and personal space and offers support, encouragement, and compassion. Remember, children depend on adults for protection.

IN A NUTSHELL...

- Educate your child on the realities of sex
- Answer questions when they occur; do not procrastinate the dialogue.
- Understand, model, and discuss healthy and appropriate boundaries.
- Give your child the right to refuse affection, hugs, or kisses from other people, and to say "NO" to unwanted touch.
- Model and support your children's feelings of empowerment.

REFLECTION

- What are your duties and responsibilities as a caregiver?
- When should you begin to talk to your child about boundaries?
- How do you plan to start the conversation with your child about sex and sexual abuse?

"IF OUR AMERICAN WAY OF LIFE FAILS THE CHILD, IT FAILS US ALL."

— **Pearl S. Buck**

TOOLS FOR YOUR CHILDREN

Teaching your children about sex from an early age equips them with tools of self-protection of their bodies and empowerment over their lives. The word "okay" is one such tool. It is the perfect word for affirmative and negative statements alike. Use this word as you train your child, and your child will learn to use it in his or her life.

"That's not okay with me." "It's okay if you hug me."

NORMAL DEVELOPMENT

As childhood development unfolds, children become curious to discover more about themselves, others, and the world around them. Participate in your children's discoveries! When parents understand this discovery process, we can become experts at providing our children with what they need to empower them about their bodies, their lives, and their relationships.

Because of their natural curiosity, children will explore sex whether you like it or not! Your responsibility is to participate in their discoveries and be the source of accurate and timely information.

Lay the foundation early so that your children can trust you and so that they can understand that sex, while natural, is something special and designed especially for an adult relationship. By taking the lead in teaching your children, you take the pressure of initiating conversations off of them, you build trust and strengthen the bond between parent and child, and you instill in your children the wisdom to recognize when someone may be trying to cross their personal boundaries.

HINTS TO HELP AVOID NEGATIVE REACTIONS:

1. Initiate age-appropriate sex talks.
2. Build trust through age-appropriate talks.
3. Avoid feelings of shame and embarrassment that you may have experienced when you were growing up and curious about sex.
4. Practice out loud if necessary.

"THE GREATEST ENEMY TO SEXUAL WHOLENESS IS SILENCE."

— **Lasser**

TEACH YOUR CHILDREN THE DIFFERENCE BETWEEN SECRETS AND SURPRISES

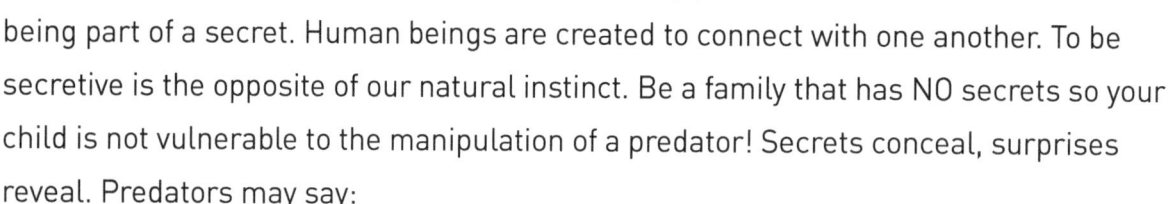

Everyone loves a surprise, and surprises are happy events that are revealed in time. But secrets denote darkness and deception. A secret is a burden on a child, and there is nothing positive about being part of a secret. Human beings are created to connect with one another. To be secretive is the opposite of our natural instinct. Be a family that has NO secrets so your child is not vulnerable to the manipulation of a predator! Secrets conceal, surprises reveal. Predators may say:

"This will be our little secret. Don't tell, because if you do, you will be punished. They may not like you anymore. They will be angry with you."

Holding the horrific secret of abuse dramatically raises a child's anxiety level, forever changing the essence of who he or she is. The secret of abuse strikes at the most intimate part of the body and soul.

Here is what you can say to your child: **"The only kinds of secrets that are okay between an adult and a child are surprises, like parties and gifts for others. Secrets that would not make someone happy are not okay to keep. Be sure and tell me if someone asks you to keep a secret because we don't keep secrets in our family."**

Caution that perpetrators will often gain trust, favoritism, and access to your child by giving gifts, treats, or special outings, and using these as the first secrets they have with kids. This is not necessarily a sad or bad secret. Stress, **"If anyone asks you to keep a secret from mommy or daddy then we need to know immediately."**

> **WHEN IT COMES TO CHILD SEXUAL ABUSE, SECRETS ARE THE MOST POWERFUL WEAPON IN A PREDATOR'S ARSENAL."**
>
> — **Jill Starishersky**

ANATOMY 101

USING APPROPRIATE TERMINOLOGY

Always use appropriate terminology when talking about body parts, emphasizing that some of these are "private parts." You begin as soon as you start teaching them the names of other body parts like eyes and ears, as early as 2 years old. Young children do not know to be embarrassed by the names of body parts. Keep your conversation simple; your young ones will accept what you tell them.

One example of a good time to begin an anatomy discussion would be during bath time and dressing. Discuss body parts and the importance of keeping the body clean, and equip them with the lesson that no one should touch their private parts. Give your little one a wash cloth to help with the bathing. "You're such a big girl! Let's wash your vagina to keep it clean and healthy."

We must teach our children correct anatomical names of their body parts. If you don't teach the correct words, then your kids will use nicknames, and in an indirect way, that creates a sense of the forbidden or something that is worth joking about. If you are uncomfortable using words like penis, vagina, and rectum, practice them until you become comfortable!

- ▶ Keep your explanations simple; don't lecture or expound on more than what a child's mind can handle.
- ▶ Become comfortable saying the words before you have conversations with your child.

PRIVATE PARTS

When naming body parts with your older toddler (2–3 years), say,
- "Some parts are private. Your penis/vagina and your rectum/etc. are not for other people to look at or touch."

As they get older, you can say:
- "It is important to tell me if anyone touches you there, even if someone tells you to keep it secret. There are no secrets between us, ever."
- "We don't talk about our private body parts in public, but I will always talk with you in private."
- "Your private parts are only to be touched and viewed for health and hygiene, like when I give my permission for a doctor and she/he has my permission to examine your private parts."

STAGES OF SEXUAL DISCOVERY

Sexual exploration and sexual discovery are natural parts of children's lives. Here are the approximate years that correlate with new behaviors and aspects of their sexual discovery.

INFANTS AND TODDLERS

- Touch is vital for the survival of infants. Touching genitals during diaper changes is normal.
- How you react—your voice, the words you use, your facial expressions—is one of your child's first lessons in sexuality. By not responding with anger, surprise, or disapproving words, you teach your child that this curiosity about his or her body is a normal part of life.

PRESCHOOL (AGES 3 TO 5)

- Many children develop a strong sense of being a boy or a girl by this age.
- Children continue to explore their bodies more intentionally.
- It is healthy to explain that touching should be done in private, not public.

- Children also become curious and want to know the answers to questions like "Where do babies come from?" and why boys and girls have different private parts. It is important to answer as honestly and clearly as possible.
- If you find your child playing doctor with another child around the same age, it's important not to overreact—to them it's just an innocent game. Of course, if an older child or adult is involved, your concern is legitimate. This may be a sign that you need to facilitate additional conversations about our bodies.

ELEMENTARY SCHOOL (AGES 6 TO 10)

- Often, children may want to play with children only of the same gender.
- Become curious about pregnancy and childbirth, especially if they (or a friend) have a younger sibling.
- Ask about conception: "How does the baby get in there, and how does it get out?"
- How to respond: "Girls are born with tiny eggs that become ready to make babies when girls are grown-ups. When a man and a woman have sex, sperm goes from the man's penis to the egg inside the woman, and together, they make a baby who grows inside the mother's womb."
- Self-touch and sex play are common.

AGES 10+

Puberty is an important time of transition for a child that creates a collision of sexual awakening, development of sex organs and body growth, and peer pressure. At this stage, remember:

- Kids still need your sensitive attention to their questions and issues about their changing bodies and sex!
- Without your attention, children turn to their peers for information about sex.
- Remain supportive of their needs.
- Stay involved and sensitive to behavioral changes throughout puberty.
- Offer lots of affirmation during this difficult stage.
- Continue to emphasize that no one should ever pressure them into any type of sexual activity.
- Keep the lines of communication open![6]

LESSON ON PRIVACY

Many young children have no inhibitions about nudity, so this is a great opportunity to introduce the concept of privacy for themselves and others. You can model the importance of privacy during bathing and using the restroom by closing the door.

You can talk about inappropriate touching by other people, BUT avoid instilling fear. You must explain to your child that even though it feels good when they touch their private parts, they can never let anyone else touch their private parts.

> "Sweetie, I know it feels good to touch your private parts. Has someone else ever touched your private parts? It's okay for you to tell me if that ever happens because that is not okay and I need to protect you."

Your child needs to understand that their private parts are only to be touched by others for health and hygiene with the permission of adults that love them.

Not just at this age but throughout your child's life, communicate openly about appropriate touch so that your child will have the tools to tell you if touching becomes inappropriate or abusive. Promotion of trust before shame and embarrassment develop allows your child the freedom to tell.

> "Mommy, Cousin Dan touched my penis and it was not okay and I screamed, 'NO' and you told me to tell you if anyone ever touched my private parts."

- ▸ You can encourage your children to trust and follow their instincts.
- ▸ Give your children permission to disobey someone if they feel uncomfortable.
- ▸ Always trust your instincts; they are 100% correct.

---

6 Dowshen, S. (2014, October 1). Understanding Early Sexual Development. Retrieved May 26, 2015, from http://kidshealth.org/parent/growth/sexual_health/development.html#.

THE BIRDS AND THE BEES: EXPLAINING SEX

"Sex is for adults who love each other. Only grown-ups should have sex with other grown-ups." Take this opportunity to share your family values and/or religious beliefs on sexual relations.

You should be clear in communicating that it is never okay for anyone, an adult or older youth, to engage in any sexual activity with a child. It is a crime.

"Like many other things that are just for adults and parents, sex is only for grownups. They show their love by being very close and sex is when a man puts his penis inside a woman's vagina."

Wait for your child's reactions because they may need or want to talk further. But always allow each child to respond individually.

And then ask...

What do you think about what I told you? Have you heard something different? Do you have any questions?

THE CONUNDRUM

Often, abusive touching feels good because sex was designed for pleasure. The victim is caught between the pleasurable feelings of sexual touching, while:

- Feeling that the abuse is wrong;
- Feeling shame, guilt and fear;
- Living in silence, hiding the trauma of abuse; and
- Possibly being threatened by the abuser.

The result is a traumatized child who drowns in silence, confusion, shame, and guilt. It is important for parents to be aware of this challenge that abused children face. Parents could take advantage of teachable moments to discuss this confusion with children and explain to them that pleasurable feelings are normal during sexual activity, even if the activity is abusive. However, although such feelings are normal, it is still not acceptable for anybody to touch them in an abusive way. Share with them that it is possible for someone they love and trust to act out abusively. Reiterate to your child that abuse is never their fault and they will not be punished if they disclose that someone has touched them inappropriately.

QUICK REVIEW: KEY PARENT-CHILD COMMUNICATION POINTS

- ▶ Be clear in communicating with your kids; it is your job to protect your children.
- ▶ Be alert for and take advantage of teachable moments.
- ▶ Be involved; be available. Involved caregivers do deter child molesters.
- ▶ Be honest with your kids in order to promote trust.
- ▶ Be encouraging to your children as you teach them to trust their instincts. Then, trust your children.
- ▶ Be clear about teaching your kids the right to say "NO" to someone (older youth or adult) if a situation feels uncomfortable.
- ▶ Trust your instincts; they are always 100% correct.
- ▶ Be aware of risky situations when your child is alone with an adult or older youth.
- ▶ You must trust and honor their instincts with affirmation by supporting their decisions to disclose unwanted touch.

ROLE PLAY EXERCISE

Write a sentence or two as though you are talking to your child about their private parts: When is it okay and not okay for others to touch their private parts? (Consider: health care workers, friends, other adults, etc.) Then practice saying it over and over until it feels conversational and you feel comfortable saying the anatomical names of their body parts.

TALKING ABOUT TOUCHING

Remember: 93% of abuse comes from someone the child knows, loves, and trusts.

Who are the people who care for your children or help with hygiene? There are many people that interact with your children: day care workers, friends, relatives, and so on.

Explain calmly to your child that others should only touch their private parts if they are helping with baths or going to the bathroom. Realize that your child may also be groomed or threatened from within your family, extended family, and close friends. Also note that both men and women sexually abuse children. This is a difficult reality to face, but one you should acknowledge.

Continue to use teachable moments to explain to your child about personal boundaries and personal power. Respecting their bodies also means that they are learning to respect others' bodies. Tell your children that it's not okay to touch or view other people's private parts, and that you need to know if someone touches or wants to see theirs. Explain that no one should touch the parts of their bodies where the bathing suit covers. Use honest and simple dialogue. **"You know that your penis is a private part, so it would not be okay for someone to show you pictures or movies of other people's penises."** Pornography is often used in grooming a child and you need to explain to your child what pornography is and why it is inappropriate to view.

IF...THEN SCENARIOS

People learn and remember principles much more readily through the use of examples. Children have wonderful imaginations, and they can be quite astute—oftentimes, far more than we give them credit. Let's look at a few examples of how you can teach your children about self-protection without fear and while using if/then statements. Note the use of the word "okay" as a tool we learned earlier. Practice scenarios so your child will know how to respond.

"If Uncle Bob tickled you in a way that made you uncomfortable, come tell me right away, okay?" or **"If Aunt Sue kissed you on the neck in a way that made you uncomfortable, it's okay for you to tell her to stop."**

Be sure your child has a plan when they feel threatened:

You can tell your child that if he/she feels threatened to:

1. Yell "NO, STOP!"
2. Run away, and
3. Tell someone.

Yell, Run, Tell is a great plan of protection to teach your child. Make sure that your child knows that they can come to you and that you will believe them.

YOU CAN ASK ME ANYTHING!

"If you ever have a question about your body, you can always ask me."

This should not be an empty promise on your part. Are you working on the computer? Are you making dinner or changing the sheets? Pause what you are doing, give your child eye contact, and listen, listen, listen! Their questions are important for both of you as you build the trust necessary to create a lasting bond about sex education.

- Don't be the parents about whom a child says: "My dad never listens." Or, "My mom is always too busy." Do be the parent who says: "If you ever have a question or feel funny about something that a person did, you can ask me about it."

- Don't freak out if the concern is about something that actually happened. Do respond with "I believe you, and I am here to protect you. Tell me more about what happened."

- Don't blow it off; don't make light of it; don't deny it. Do respond by listening, believing, and discussing. If you respond in any other way, then you have created the first step in causing your child to feel shame and guilt, a decrease in self-worth and self-esteem, and your child will think twice about ever talking to you again about a life-changing experience.

Remember: It's your job to support your children and keep them safe.

Giving your child a backup plan is also important:

"If you ever have a question that you can't ask me, be sure to ask (NAME SOMEONE CLOSE) because I trust him/her, and I know s/he will help you."

STRATEGIES

Strategy 1: Make a pact with your child. Tell them that if they want to talk about something difficult, they can show you some sort of behavior, such as putting a teddy bear on your pillow.

> "Honey, let's make a deal. If you ever want to talk to me about something that is difficult, or you are embarrassed to use the words, take your (teddy bear) and put it on my bed by my pillow. When I see your (teddy bear) on the bed, I will know that you need to talk to me privately about something important. I will come get you and we can talk about whatever it is you need to discuss. Is that a deal?"

Strategy 2: Learn the behavioral signs of child sexual abuse, and ask your child directly if anyone has ever touched their private parts or asked them to touch theirs. The most telling sign of CSA is a drastic unexplainable change in behavior, sexual language and/or behavior that is not age-appropriate, chronic stomach aches, and headaches.

ONE-ON-ONE CHILD-ADULT INTERACTION

Teach your child to be aware of their surroundings when they are one-on-one with adults. For example, your child should never be alone with a teacher when the door is closed. What other scenarios might you include here? Consider music lessons, private tutoring, faith-based events, extended family visits, etc. Also be aware at family functions—like weddings, reunions, or funerals—when a child can be lured away from a crowd. Drop in unexpectedly to let your child know you are always protecting them.

DENIAL

Here is an important fact to keep in mind: most children will deny the molestation occurred the first time (and possibly several times) you ask them.

Children are loyal and trusting; they want to please people. They don't want to be troublemakers, but reporting someone who molested them is far different than telling on the person who threw a rock or took a toy at school. Molestation is intimate and traumatizing; it is an event that far exceeds a child's maturity level of understanding— except to know that it is wrong.

Therefore, you must continually give your child permission, and in the process, the confidence to tell you when something bad happens, even if Grandpa, Aunt Suzie, or big brother are involved.

Stress that you are doing your job of protecting your child, not looking to hurt anyone else. Remember your commitment? "It's my job to support you and keep you safe."

Remaining involved and interested in your children's lives will go a long way in building the foundation of the trust your kids have in you. You don't always have to have heavy and uncomfortable conversations about abuse or sex in order to build their self-esteem. You can have relaxed age appropriate, layered conversations that become *"teachable moments"* to protect and empower your child.

BE SURE YOUR KIDS UNDERSTAND:

- "No matter what anybody tells you, I will always believe you if you tell me that someone has done something to you that is not okay."
- "No matter what anyone tells you, I will protect you and you will never be in trouble for something that another person does to you."
- "No one, not even adults and older kids that you know, should do or say things that make you feel uncomfortable. Tell me immediately."
- "I am an adult, and I can protect myself against any threats."

IN A NUTSHELL

The tough talk involves:
1. Layers of conversations over time
2. Clinical information about sex
3. A tool for self-protection and awareness
4. Foundations for establishing healthy relationships
5. Your parental duty and responsibility

- Communication during non-threatening moments makes conversations easier during difficult times.
- Everyday activities can present discussion opportunities in relaxed and casual conversation.
- These discussions are times to reinforce family values and build trust.
- Be familiar with behavioral signs of child sexual abuse.

POTENTIAL SIGNS OF CHILD SEXUAL ABUSE

Parents and guardians should be alert to the potential indicators of sexual abuse:

- Changes in behavior, mood swings, withdrawal, anxiety, fearfulness, and excessive crying
- Bed-wetting, nightmares, fear of going to bed, or other sleep disturbances
- Acting out inappropriate sexual activity, showing an unusual interest in sexual matters, or having sexual knowledge and language beyond their years
- A sudden acting out of feelings or aggressive or rebellious behavior

- Regression to infantile behavior and clinging
- A fear of certain places, people, or activities
- Pain, itching, bleeding, fluid, or rawness in private areas of a child's body
- Eating disorders—bulimia, anorexia, or overeating
- Harming themselves physically—i.e., burning or cutting

If you observe any of these potential indicators in your children, talk to them about the causes. Changes like these may be due to causes other than sexual exploitation, such as a medical, family, or school problem. Be sure to work with your child to get to the root of the problem. Also, keep in mind that children do not always demonstrate obvious signs such as these, but may do or say something that hints at sexual abuse. Always be mindful of a drastic change in behavior that cannot be explained.

WHO ARE THE PERPETRATORS?

Ninety-three percent of all sexual abusers are acquaintances or family members, trusted and loved by their victims.[7]

> That translates to only 7% of abusers as strangers.
>
> 1 in 5 children under age 12 is assaulted by fathers/stepfathers.

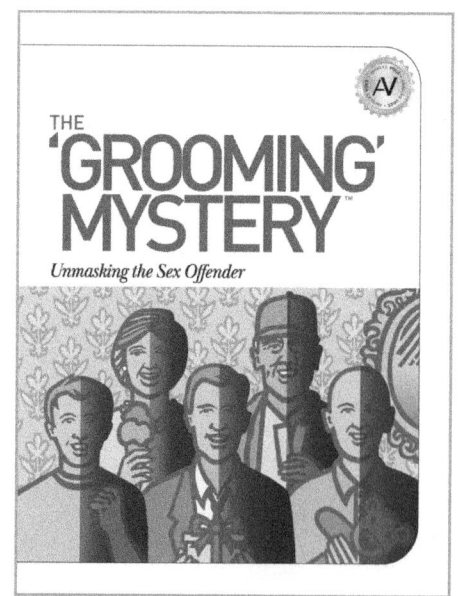

Perpetrators take advantage of these relationships to exert power over and to control their victims. Children are vulnerable and easily manipulated. It is devastating to think that someone close to you or your family would sexually violate your child, but you must accept that the greatest risk of sexual abuse is by someone you and your child know and trust.

To learn more about perpetrators and the grooming process please read, *The 'Grooming' Mystery*, published by Angela's Voice.

---

[7] U.S. Bureau of Justice Statistics. 2000 Sexual Assault of Young Children as Reported to Law Enforcement. 2000.

DISCLOSURE

The following pages outline the steps that you need to take if your child discloses to you that s/he has been sexually assaulted. This will certainly be a difficult and traumatizing experience for you, but it is vital that you support your child in the best way that you possibly can.

> "No matter how prosperous a nation, how developed, all share the plight and embarrassment of having so many suffering children. We are united by our neglect, our abuse, our absence of love. Have we forgotten about the children, and thus forsaken the next generation?"
>
> — **Audrey Hepburn**

CALMLY RECEIVING A DISCLOSURE

- ▶ Listen to the child carefully and write down what you hear so that you can report the facts to the authorities.
- ▶ Do not coach the child; do not suggest answers.
- ▶ Do not ask questions seeking more information. Let the child talk freely of his or her own volition. Children typically repeat the story accurately one time.
- ▶ Document what your child says.
- ▶ Report everything you know, even if—especially if—the predator is in your home.
- ▶ Let authorities manage the situation while you care for the child.
- ▶ Say: "I believe you, and I will do everything I can to protect you. You did the right thing by telling me. I'm proud of you. This is not your fault."

DISCLOSURE—UNDERSTANDING THE PROCESS

- Child Sexual Abuse is a CRIME! IMMEDIATELY CALL 911!
- Always report suspicions of child sexual abuse.
- While seeking justice by reporting to authorities, advocate for the child.

FOLLOWING A DISCLOSURE

- Immediately remove your child from the dangerous environment.
- Document all evidence of abuse. Prosecuting child sexual abuse cases can be extremely difficult, so it is vital to preserve any evidence of the abuse.
- Report to local law enforcement or child protective services.
- Contact a local Child Advocacy Center for guidance.
- Use and depend on the help of others.
- Understand a formal investigation will occur before any action is taken.
- Be courageous and advocate for the child.

BE AWARE AND PREPARE

- You will probably be required to provide a statement of what the child told you.
- Use what you wrote down and be specific.
- The justice system may be frustrating with long waits or professionals who may not be immediately responsive.

FOCUS ON THE FACT THAT YOUR CHILD IS NOW SAFE

- Children are frequently asked to testify in cases of sexual abuse. Do not be afraid or shy about procuring counseling for your child, yourself, or your family. Professional help is vital to recovery.

CHILD ADVOCACY CENTERS

Child Advocacy Centers are child-friendly, central locations for trauma intervention that may provide some or all of these services:

- Crisis Services: intervention, assessment, and treatment
- Forensic Services: interviews and evaluations
- Mental Health Services: evaluations, examinations, and individual and group counseling
- Medical Services: examinations, evaluations, and referrals
- Advocacy Services: family and court advocacy

MORE CAC SERVICES

- Case Tracking Services: collection and maintenance of appropriate data in a central location
- Training Services: for private, public, and community partners
- Prevention Services: education and prevention provided to our private, public, and community partners

DON'T FORGET TO TAKE CARE OF YOURSELF

Finding out that your child has experienced sexual abuse is an extraordinarily upsetting discovery. While your primary duties are to ensure that your child is out of harm's way and to help them seek the help that they need, do not forget that you may need to seek out support for yourself as well. Seek counseling or reach out to a local child advocacy center for support.

REFERENCES

Black, M. C., Basile, K. C., Breiding, M. J., Smith, S. G., Walters, M. L., Merrick, M. T., Chen, J., & Stevens,

Centers for Disease Control and Prevention. (2013). Retrieved from www.cdc.gov/nccdphp/ace/findings.html.

Child Sexual Abuse. (2009, January 1). Retrieved May 4, 2015, from http://www.rainn.org/get-information/types-of-sexual-assault/child-sexual-abuse.

Child Sexual Abuse (n.d.). Retrieved May 4, 2015, from http://www.americanhumane.org/children/stop-child-abuse/fact-sheets/child-sexual- abuse.html.

Darkness to Light. (2007). Retrieved from www.d2l.org/KnowAbout/statistics_2.asp.

Laaser, M. (1999). Talking to your kids about sex. New York: Waterbrook.

M. R. (2011). National Intimate Partner and Sexual Violence Survey: 2010 summary report.

Retrieved from the Centers for Disease Control and Prevention, National Center for Injury Prevention and Control: http://www.cdc.gov/ViolencePrevention/pdf/NISVS_Report2010-a.pdf.

Saul J, Audage NC. Preventing Child Sexual Abuse Within Youth-serving Organizations: Getting Started on Policies and Procedures. Atlanta (GA): Centers for Disease Control and Prevention, National Center for Injury Prevention and Control; 2007.

Sexual Revictimization Research Brief. (2012). Retrieved May 4, 2015, from https://nsvrc.org/sites/defalt/files/publications_NSVRC_ResearchBrief_Sexual- Revictimization .pdf.

RECOMMENDED BOOKS

ON SEX

Beyond the Birds and the Bees:
Fostering Your Child's Healthy Sexual
Development in Today's World
By Beverly Engel

How to Talk to Your Child About Sex:
It's Best to Start Early, but It's Never too Late—
a Step-by-Step Guide for Every Age
By Linda Eyre and Richard Eyre

Sex Without Shame:
Encouraging the Child's Healthy
Sexual Development
By Alayne Yates

What's the Big Secret?:
Talking about Sex with Girls and Boys
By Laurie Krasny Brown and Marc Brown

Where Did I Come From?:
The facts of life without any nonsense
and with illustrations
By Peter Mayle

ON SEX ABUSE

My Body Belongs to Me
By Jill Starishevsky

A Very Touching Book...for Little People
and for Big People
By Jan Hindman

Fred the Fox Shouts "No!"
By Tatiana Y. Kisil Matthews

It's My Body
By Lory Freeman

My Body Is Private
By Linda Walvoord Girard, Rodney Pate
(Illustrator)

Some Secrets Should Never Be Kept
By Jayneen Sanders

Telling Isn't Tattling
By Kathryn M. Hammerseng

The Right Touch: A Read Aloud Story to Help
Prevent Child Sexual Abuse
By Sandy Kleven,
Jody Lynn Bergsma (Illustrator)

When I Was Little Like You
By Jane Porett

Angela's Voice

Angela's Voice is dedicated to developing, distributing, and endorsing valuable resources in the awareness, prevention, and healing of child sexual abuse. The materials, though specific for survivors of child sexual abuse, also benefit any abuse survivor and help protect children by teaching them how to defend themselves from abusive behavior. Founder Angela Williams, MFP, is a survivor-turned-advocate who shares a powerful message of triumph over tragedy by sharing her vulnerable and candid voice about her abuse trauma, her pain, her struggles, and her journey to healing in hopes that it may help other survivors expedite their healing journey.

Williams has devoted years to providing awareness, prevention, and healing programs through her advocacy work. Williams has captivated audiences with her powerful message of triumph over tragedy as a victim of childhood physical and sexual abuse. At age seventeen, she attempted suicide, and that day was the end of her torment and the beginning of a journey to healing. She is a crusader for change and dedicates her life to eradicate child sexual abuse. She holds a master's in forensic psychology with a concentration in child abuse. Williams is a powerful messenger, appearing in national and international news and documentaries. She has been successful in state legislative reform and national policy work and served on the Policy Committee of the National Coalition to Prevent Child Sexual Abuse and Exploitation. She has received numerous accolades and awards for her work, including her collection of books that have valuable lessons for survivors of all ages.

Please follow Angela Williams on social media and contact angelasvoice.com to book a speaking event or interview.

Books by Angela Williams

Loving Me: After Abuse
From Sorrows to Sapphires, Angela Williams's Memoir

Interactive Workbooks—Adults

<u>Healing</u>
Pathway to Healing, Guide to Healing
True Intimacy
Shattering the Shame
Unveiling Child Sexual Abuse

<u>Prevention</u>
Tough Talk to Tender Hearts
The Grooming Mystery
Single Parenting Solutions
Courage to Speak

Children's Books (Ages 5–10)
Gracie Finds Her Voice
Grant Gets His Shield
Gracie and Grant's Big Win
Gracie and Grant's Big Win Coloring Book
Find Your Voice Curriculum Book

Join the Angela's Voice Movement

Take action to break the silence and cycle of Child Sexual Abuse and Exploitation

HELP US SAVE THE NEXT GENERATION OF CHILDREN!

1. Be a Child Advocate
2. Donate at angelasvoice.com
3. Invite Angela Williams to Speak
4. Purchase another Angela's Voice Prevention or Healing Book

Discover more child sexual abuse prevention and healing resources at angelasvoice.com and follow angelasvoice in social media.

Instagram @Angelasvoice

Facebook @Angelasvoice

Twitter @Angelasvoice

Linkedin/angelasvoice

Angelasvoice.blogspot.com

Youtube.com/angelakwilliams

FACILITATION GUIDE

FACILITATION GUIDE: TOUGH TALK TO TENDER HEARTS

Tough Talk To Tender Hearts is designed for both self-study and group study. Incorporating group study allows you to break down the barriers of communication related to the issue of child sexual abuse (CSA) and gives adults an open forum to discuss fears and concerns surrounding the issue of CSA. The program is written to be easily facilitated with an accompanying PowerPoint presentation to offer key points of the training. Angela's Voice seeks to provide opportunities for the lessons in *Tough Talk To Tender Hearts* to be shared outside of the training session and taught in your community.

Visit **angelasvoice.com/toughtalk** to download the Facilitators PowerPoint.

The following provides tips to help you with facilitation. Angela's Voice hopes to help you in the planning and implementation of your program. By teaching the subsequent prevention information, you will offer your community valuable information to protect the welfare and safety of its children.

LOGISTICS

The success of any group facilitation relies on good planning and organization. We recommend that you schedule your training program at least four weeks prior to the event. For a successful training, secure a location to accommodate the number in your class. Depending on the size of your group, training could be held in your home, your church, or a community resource center. Make sure you have your location, date, and time secured in writing during week 1 of planning.

MARKETING

Create a printed flyer. Pertinent information to include:

- Program Description: Tough Talk To Tender Hearts
- Date
- Location
- Time
- Registration Instructions

Great marketing tools for your training include posters, flyers, print media, newsletters, and social media. You could email Angela's Voice at angela@angelakwilliams.com if you would like to add your training to the monthly calendar on the Angela's Voice website. All marketing distribution should be completed during week 2 of planning.

PREPARATION

Discussing the sensitive topic of CSA is challenging. Spend time becoming familiar with the content prior to organizing a training session. You can utilize the PowerPoint presentation provided by Angela's Voice to assist you in facilitating the program, or you can use the books to supplement your facilitation in a smaller, more intimate gathering. Practice facilitating the information with your family or a small group prior to your presentation.

It is important to prepare a referral resource handout (referral network) for anyone in your audience that may be struggling with a personal issue related to CSA. This list should include the name, email and phone number of the local child advocacy center and a list of three mental health professionals in your community that treat survivors of child sexual abuse. All preparation proceeding the training session should be completed during week 2 of planning.

OBJECTIVES

By the end of the training, participants should be able to:

1. Demonstrate the enormity of child sexual abuse through identifying the facts about CSA;
2. Talk with their children about sex using anatomically-correct language;
3. Talk with their children about how to establish boundaries; and
4. Identify potential signs of child sexual abuse

We hope that parents will develop the intention to discuss these important issues with their children. In order to achieve these objectives, ask participants throughout the training if their knowledge, beliefs, and/or intentions have shifted due to reading about and discussing CSA.

DISCUSSION GUIDELINES

As you know, the topic of CSA is extremely sensitive. In order to help make discussions run as smoothly as possible, the following are some discussion guidelines for you as a facilitator:

1. Have the group set common ground rules to help create a safe environment where everyone feels comfortable sharing and participating. Example ground rules can include:

    a. Participate/don't dominate

    b. Practice self-care

    c. Practice active listening

    d. Minimize cell phone usage and other distractions

2. Use open-ended questions such as "What do you think?" or "What are some of your ideas?"

3. Maintain an unconditionally positive regard for each participant.

4. Avoid the temptation of providing all of the answers to the participants. We learn and retain information better when we come up with the answers ourselves. Everyone has something valuable to share!

5. Be attentive and recap main points that were made by others when the opportunity permits.

6. Try not to let a small group or one person (including yourself) dominate the discussion. Remind participants that they agreed to the ground rule "participate/don't dominate" and ask quieter participants for their views.

7. Serve as a role model for the group on how to be flexible and open to the ideas of others.

DISCLOSURE

If someone discloses that they suspect abuse of a child, it is imperative that you encourage them to call child protective services or law enforcement to report the abuse. In addition, if someone discloses that they are a victim of CSA and are struggling, please refer them to your referral network mentioned in the "Preparation" section above. It is important for you to emphasize the urgency of reporting CSA to those who attend your training session. If a child is shot and bleeding we don't delay; we seek immediate assistance. The same urgency must be taken with suspicions of child sexual abuse.

As a resource, please download and print copies of the "REPORT NOW" (angelasvoice.com/reportnow) brochure to distribute during your training. Additionally, the Angela's Voice website contains many resources for you to share with your audience.

FACILITATOR PRESENTATION TIPS

Below are some helpful tips that could be useful for your presentation during the training session. These tips are elaborated upon in the PowerPoint presentation that supplements this guide.

- ▶ Practice being a good listener
- ▶ Use inclusive pronouns such as "we" and "our"
- ▶ Use a conversational tone when appropriate
- ▶ Give information when appropriate
- ▶ Incorporate personal experience (yours and theirs)
- ▶ Get to know your audience—allow time for introductions and icebreakers
- ▶ Use appropriate body language
- ▶ Give a brief overview of the purpose of the training
- ▶ Establish appropriate eye contact
- ▶ Shake hands when group is small and intimate
- ▶ Adapt your presenting style based on group's response
- ▶ Be mindful of timing

RESEARCH AND DEVELOPMENT

Angela's Voice is consistently evaluating participants' experiences to ensure that *Tough Talk To Tender Hearts* is accomplishing its goals.

1. Have all participants sign the log to maintain a database of those who have completed the *Tough Talk To Tender Hearts* Training.
   Email the sign-in log to angela@angelakwilliams.com within 7 days of the training date.

2. Complete and distribute the Certificate of Completion for each participant at angelasvoice.com/toughtalk.

3. Have participants complete pre and post survey evaluations. The evaluations can be found at the back of each workbook as well as online. In order to get the evaluations back to us, you can do one of the following:
   - **Scan them.** Fill out the evaluations by hand and scan them to angela@angelakwilliams.com.
   - **Fill them out online.** You can find the evaluations online at:
     - Pre-test: https://goo.gl/4tBTMT
     - Post-Test: https://goo.gl/Rj2JWU

Angela's Voice is grateful for your hard work and dedication to helping facilitate CSA prevention training in your home and your community. If you have additional questions please don't hesitate to contact Angela's Voice at angela@angelakwilliams.com or visit our website angelasvoice.com.

PRE-WORKSHOP QUESTIONNAIRE

ID: _____
Date: _____

Instructions: Please answer the following questions to the best of your ability. These questions are meant to reflect your opinions and experiences.

1. How old are you? _____ years

2. What is your gender? _____

3. What are the ages and genders of your children?

	Child 1	Child 2	Child 3	Child 4	Child 5
Age					
Gender	M / F	M / F	M / F	M / F	M / F

4. What race do you consider yourself to be?
   - ☐ Asian / Pacific Islander
   - ☐ Black / African American
   - ☐ Hispanic / Latin(o/a)
   - ☐ Native American / Alaskan
   - ☐ White
   - ☐ Other: _____

5. What is your family's annual household income?
   - ☐ Less than $10,000
   - ☐ $10,001 to $20,000
   - ☐ $20,001 to $40,000
   - ☐ $41,001 to $60,000
   - ☐ $60,001 to $80,000
   - ☐ $80,001 to $100,000
   - ☐ More than $100,000

6. What is your religious affiliation? _____

7. Have you discussed child sexual abuse with your child(ren)?
   - ☐ Yes
   - ☐ No

8. If yes, in what context have you taught your child(ren) about sexual abuse? (check all that apply)
   - ☐ Home
   - ☐ School
   - ☐ Community Organizations
   - ☐ Religious group / a place of worship
   - ☐ Other: _____

9. If no, why not?
   - ☐ I do not believe my child is in danger.
   - ☐ I believe my child is too young.
   - ☐ My child has learned about sexual abuse in another context.
   - ☐ Other: _____

10. In your opinion, at what age should children learn about sexual abuse? _____ years

11. What topics have you previously discussed with your child(ren)? (check all that apply)
    - ☐ Someone might try to lure you into their car
    - ☐ Someone might try to touch your "private parts"
    - ☐ Someone might try to touch your "private parts" and ask you to keep it a secret
    - ☐ Someone might try to tempt you with rewards
    - ☐ Someone might try to touch your "private parts" with an object
    - ☐ Someone might try to show you their "private parts"
    - ☐ Someone might ask you to touch their "private parts"
    - ☐ Other: _____
    - ☐ I have not previously discussed these topics with my child(ren)

12. Who have you discussed with your child(ren) as a potential abuser? (check all that apply)
    - ☐ Strangers
    - ☐ Adults your child(ren) knows
    - ☐ Older children or adolescents
    - ☐ Relatives
    - ☐ Siblings
    - ☐ Parents
    - ☐ Other: _____
    - ☐ I have not previously discussed these topics with my child(ren)

Please indicate your agreement with the following statements on a scale of 1 (Strongly Disagree) to 5 (Strongly Agree)

	(1) Strongly Disagree	(2) Disagree	(3) Neutral	(4) Agree	(5) Strongly Agree
Child abuse includes only touching.					
Most children are sexually abused by people not well known to the child.					
Child sexual abuse takes place in mainly poor, disorganized, unstable families.					
The majority of perpetrators use physical force to sexually abuse children.					
Most perpetrators are trusted by the child.					
Most perpetrators tell the child to keep the abuse a secret and threaten the child not to tell.					
Parents should wait to talk to their child(ren) about sex until they have reached puberty.					
Parents should talk to their child(ren) repeatedly throughout their childhood and adolescence.					
Parents should use correct anatomical terms for body parts when speaking to their child(ren).					
Children should always be expected to allow relatives or family friends to hug and kiss them, even if they do not want to be touched.					
Parents should model appropriate personal boundaries in the home.					

Below, please indicate how often you have done the following in the last 30 days:

In the last 30 days, how often have you....

	Never (0 times)	Sometimes (1-5 times)	Often (6 or more times)
Talked with your child(ren) about the dangers of sexual abuse?			
Talked with your child(ren) about the differences between safe and unsafe touches?			
Told your child(ren) that other people should only touch his/her private parts to keep them clean and healthy?			
Assured your child(ren) that sexual abuse is never his/her fault?			
Told your child(ren) never to keep secrets about inappropriate touching?			
Talked with your child(ren) about what to do if another person asks to touch his/her private parts?			
Modeled or talked about privacy in your home?			
Used anatomically correct terms for genitals when talking to your child(ren)?			

Below, please indicate how confident you are...

	(1) Not very confident	(2) Not confident	(3) Neutral	(4) Confident	(5) Very Confident
Talking with your child(ren) about sexual education in a healthy and age appropriate way.					
Talking with your child(ren) about the dangers of child sexual abuse.					
Using anatomically correct terms for genitalia when talking to your child(ren).					

POST-WORKSHOP QUESTIONNAIRE

ID: _____
Date: _____

Instructions: Please answer the following questions to the best of your ability. These questions are meant to reflect your opinions and experiences.

In your opinion, at what age should children learn about sexual abuse? _____ years

Please indicate your agreement with the following statements on a scale of 1 (Strongly Disagree) to 5 (Strongly Agree)

	(1) Strongly Disagree	(2) Disagree	(3) Neutral	(4) Agree	(5) Strongly Agree
Child abuse includes only touching.					
Most children are sexually abused by strangers.					
Child sexual abuse takes place in mainly poor, disorganized, unstable families.					
The majority of perpetrators use physical force to sexually abuse children.					
Most perpetrators are trusted by the child.					
Most perpetrators tell the child to keep the abuse a secret and threaten the child not to tell.					
Parents should wait to talk to their child(ren) about sex until they have reached puberty.					
Parents should talk to their child(ren) repeatedly throughout their childhood and adolescence.					
Parents should use correct anatomical terms for body parts when speaking to their child(ren).					
Children should always be expected to allow relatives or family friends to hug and kiss them, even if they do not want to be touched.					
Parents should model appropriate personal boundaries in the home.					

Please indicate how confident you are...

	(1) Not very confident	(2) Not confident	(3) Neutral	(4) Confident	(5) Very Confident
Talking with your child(ren) about sexual education in a healthy and age appropriate way.					
Talking with your child(ren) about the dangers of child sexual abuse.					
Using anatomically correct terms for genitalia when talking to your child(ren).					

FOLLOW-UP QUESTIONNAIRE

ID: _____
Date: _____

Instructions: Please answer the following questions to the best of your ability. These questions are meant to reflect your opinions and experiences.

Below, please indicate how often you have done the following since the workshop (within the last 60 days):

		Never (0 times)	Sometimes (1-5 times)	Often (6 or more times)
1.	Asked your child(ren) to use his/her "NO!" voice before going out to play or any other time.			
2.	Talked to your child(ren) about sex using anatomically correct terms for his/her genitals.			
3.	Talked to your child(ren) about the differences between safe and unsafe touches.			
4.	Told your child(ren) that it is okay to say "No" to someone's touch if it feels uncomfortable to them, even if it is a family member or friend.			

5. Within the last 60 days, has your child(ren) told you or anyone else about a touch or situation that made them feel uncomfortable?

   ☐ Yes

   ☐ No

   If you responded with "no," you have completed this assessment.
   If you responded with "yes," please answer the following questions.

6. How did you handle this situation? _____
   _____
   _____
   _____.

7. What resources did you use?
   ☐ Child Advocacy Center
   ☐ Rape crisis center
   ☐ Mental health services
   ☐ Hospital
   ☐ Case tracking service
   ☐ Police Department
   ☐ Other: _____

8. Did you report the case?
   ☐ Yes
   ☐ No
   ☐ Prefer not to say

Ingram Content Group UK Ltd.
Milton Keynes UK
UKHW050625170523
421881UK00007B/33